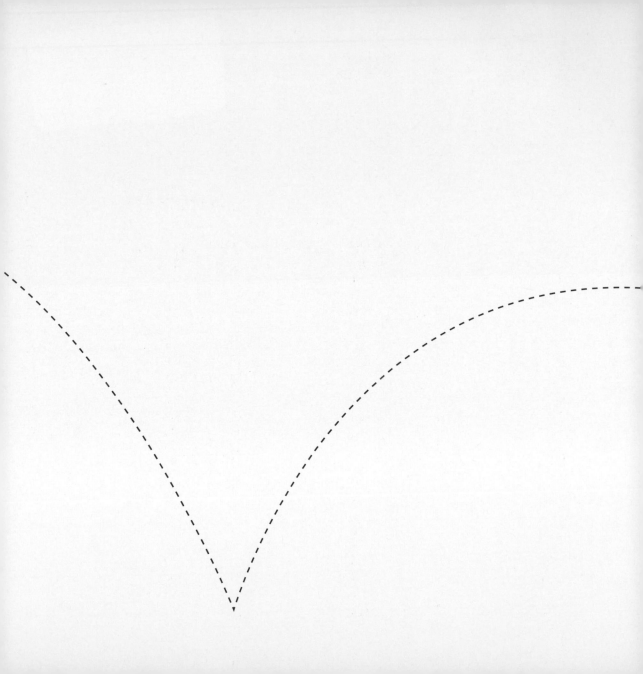

DINK!

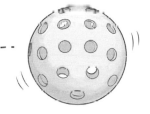

Pickleball Facts, Fictions, and Cartoons

Ellis Rosen

UNION
SQUARE
& CO.

NEW YORK

UNION SQUARE & CO.

NEW YORK

For Meghan, Sadie, and Max.

ISBN 978-1-4549-4762-2 (hardcover)
ISBN 978-1-4549-4763-9 (e-book)

For information about custom editions, special sales, and premium purchases, please contact specialsales@unionsquareandco.com.

Printed in China

2 4 6 8 10 9 7 5 3 1

unionsquareandco.com

Cover design by Melissa Farris
Interior design by Gavin Motnyk

Contents

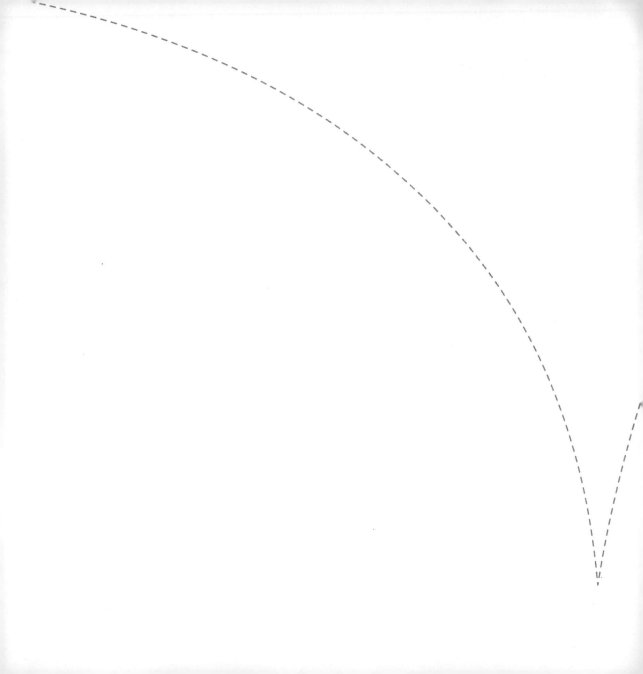

INTRODUCTION FOR PICKLEBALL PLAYERS

Hello. This is the introduction for people who already play pickleball. If you do not play pickleball, please turn to page 5 for the introduction for people who have not played pickleball. Read that, then go outside and play a minimum of, oh, I don't know, twenty, thirty games? Enough to get the feel of it. Then come back and read this introduction. I'll wait.

Back? Great! It's fun, right? Okay, now that you are a pickleball player we can talk about all the exciting things this book has in store for you. First off, let me just say this right away: this book *will* make you a better pickleball player.* Cool, right? Also, this book will make you laugh. Well, hopefully. Humor is subjective, and it's possible that your sense of humor sucks. If you do not find it funny, I only ask that you do not go on Goodreads, give this one star, and

---

*Legally speaking, this book will absolutely not make you a better pickleball player.

make a rude comment about how unfunny this book is. My mom is on Goodreads and she might see it.

Here's what's in this book: cartoons, humor, do's and don'ts, jokes, funny stuff that defies definition—and all of it will be related to pickleball. There's going to be a glossary of terms. There's going to be diagrams and pro tips. Are there going to be jokes about golf? No! This is a pickleball book—try to keep up.

If you're after a step-by-step guide to practicing your swing, with photographs of people demonstrating each position, this isn't the book you're looking for. I'm sure someone has made that book. It's not too late: you can still put this book down, walk to the "sports" section of the bookstore, and read the introduction for that one. Let me know if it's any good!

"Hey, after this, do you want to walk into a bar?"

Anyway, you're probably wondering why the mix of pickleball and humor. I believe the two are intrinsically linked. Pickleball is a funny sport. For instance, it's called "pickleball." Also, it's a hybrid sport that was literally created with stuff that was just lying around. We call it a "hybrid sport," but let's be real: pickleball is the improv comedy of sports. If tennis is the older, serious sibling, pickleball is the loud, funny kid that no one pays much attention to.

This is not to say that you, seasoned pickleball player, do not take the sport seriously! Of course you do. You're very good, all that practicing has paid off, everyone is talking about your serve. But that's the beauty of the sport! Pickleball players take the game, not themselves, seriously. Now, I am not a seasoned pickleball player, but I am a professional cartoonist, and I can say with all the amount of confidence a meek guy like me can muster: cartooning is the same. Cartoonists take the medium, but not ourselves, seriously. We are the pickleball players of art—or, to continue this series of confusing analogies, we are the improv comedy of sports of art. Or something. I need an editor.

The point I'm getting at is that humor and pickleball are a match made in heaven—and if you don't believe me, read this book. If you still don't believe me after reading it, just remember my mom is on Goodreads.

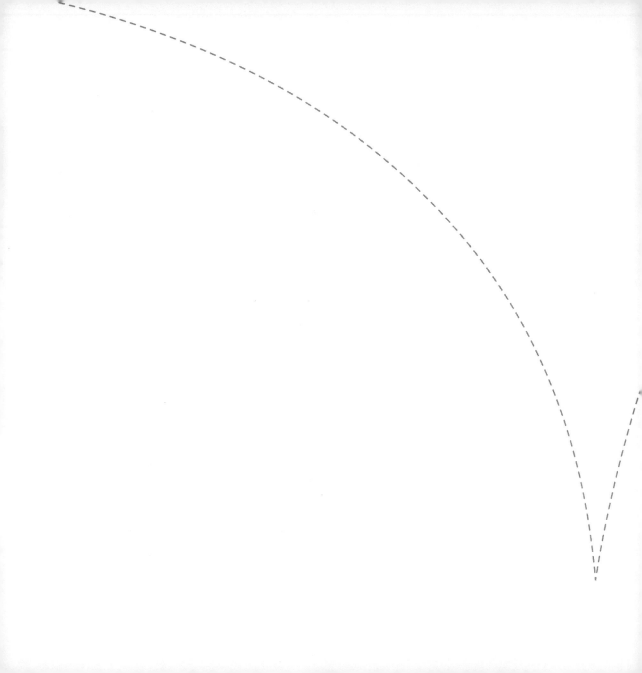

INTRODUCTION FOR NON-PICKLEBALL PLAYERS

Hello. This is the introduction for people who have never played pickleball. I'm not quite sure why you have picked up this book. My guess is that you're currently perusing the shelves in a bookstore and the cover caught your eye. Maybe the title intrigued you. Maybe you've always wanted to know about pickleball but didn't want to ask your uncle about it because you know he'll never shut up and you'll have to stand there, listening to him go on and on, not really paying attention but politely nodding along anyway, waiting for something to distract him so you can slip away. Regardless, you're reading this now, and that means you must have some slight interest in pickleball, or at least a passing curiosity. Great! I'm glad you're here.

If you're reading this because you hope it will teach you how to play, well . . . I mean, sure, maybe. But if you really want to learn to play, I suggest you go out and actually play the game. Playing it really is the best way to learn, but reading about it is a close second. However, despite that, I do not suggest trying both at the same time.

You may have noticed that there is an introduction in this book for people who *do* play. If you have played pickleball and consider yourself familiar with it, that introduction might be more your speed. This intro is going to take it nice and slow. Let's begin.

pick·le·ball
/ˈpik(ə)lˌbôl/

Following me so far? Great, let's continue. If you have heard anything about pickleball, it's this: pickleball is America's fastest-growing sport. You'll hear that everywhere. People go from curious to cultlike acolytes within days. Old or young, if you try to pick up pickleball, chances are you'll become really annoying about it.

Why? Well, for one, it's easy. Anyone can play, and because pickleball doesn't require great herculean fits of strength, anyone can enjoy it. It's a fun social game with lots of silly vocabulary and goofy outcomes.

"It's Zeus's latest obsession."

Okay, that was a lot of information! Let's take a little break. Take a deep breath. Seen any good TV lately? I just started watching *Severance*. It's really good!

Ready to get back to it? Pickleball is a paddleball sport that combines elements of badminton, table tennis, and tennis. Two to four players play on a court that usually measures twenty by forty-four feet. Players use short-handled paddles to hit a perforated plastic ball over a low net.

The game is played similarly to tennis but with several modifications. I'm not going to get into the rules, as that would be boring and unhelpful. Like I said, if you want to learn how to play, leave this bookstore and go out and play! Please put this book down on the "best sellers" table on your way out.

If you're still here, let me tell you what this book is about. I'm going to copy and paste this section from the Introduction for Players, because it works for both sections and I can be lazy: this book will contain cartoons, humor, do's and don'ts, jokes, and funny stuff that defies definition, and all of it will be related to pickleball. There's going to be a glossary of terms. There's going to be diagrams and pro tips.

In other words, if you like cartoons and jokes, then maybe you'll put up with all the pickleball stuff. You might even learn enough about the sport to get in a word or two when talking to your uncle. Probably not. That guy is not a good listener. Anyway, my hope is that after reading this, you'll try playing pickleball yourself. The more people who play the game, the easier it will be to sell a follow-up to this book. Maybe your uncle will even buy it.

Cartoon Interlude 1

"One more game, then we'll get on the ark."

THE POPULARITY OF PICKLEBALL INSPIRES A NEW WAVE OF HYBRID SPORTS:

FENCHERY
Fencing + Archery

BUCKET LIST BALL
Basketball + Skydiving

PROCRASTIBALL
*Any Sport + Checking Your
Phone Every 5 Seconds*

"That's what I love about the game—it's so social."

"You should try fetch with a pickleball.
It's easier on the knees."

"Ok, one more game, but then we really have to get back to the invasion."

Captain Ahab and Moby Dick in Retirement

"Can this wait? I'm in the middle of a
game with the dove."

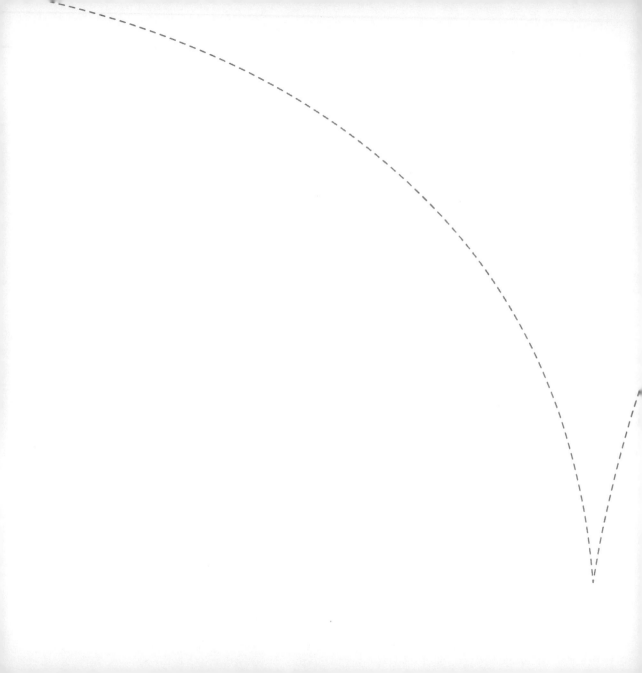

THE PICKLEBALL GLOSSARY

As we discussed in the Introduction—which of course you read, because what kind of person skips the Introduction? certainly not you—you're probably already familiar with pickleball. But because this is a pickleball book, it should have a glossary of pickleball terms, and it just so happens that I need to fill up more pages with content and my editor told me I can't make the font any bigger, which is, frankly, ridiculous, Kate.

Anyway, I'm currently sitting at a booth in my favorite diner, my phone is dead, and the waiter won't make eye contact with me, so I figure now is as good a time as any to write down some important pickleball terms. For simplicity's sake, I have divided this glossary into three parts: "Things You Need to Know," "Things You Don't Necessarily Need to Know but Probably Should," and "Things You Don't Need to Know, but What the Hell, Here they Are Anyway." There is technically a fourth category: "Things You Do Not Want to Know, Trust Me," but I'm going to leave that out for your own safety.

Things You Need to Know

The Pickleball

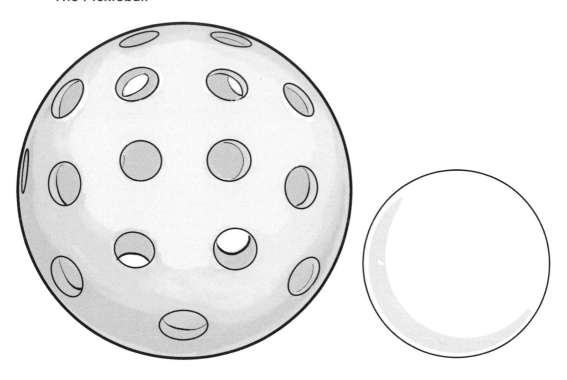

This is a picture of a
pickleball (actual size).

This is a picture of a Ping-Pong ball
for comparison (actual size).

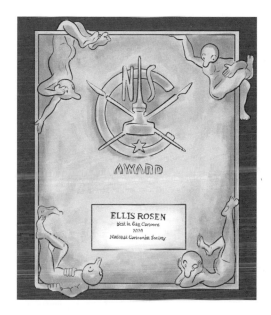

Here is a picture of an award I got for cartooning
(not actual size, the real one is much bigger).

You may think that a pickleball is very similar to a Wiffle ball. You would be right. The size and weight are nearly identical. If you were playing pickleball with a Wiffle ball, the game would be unchanged, unlike, say, if you were playing pickleball with a bowling ball. Trust me, I've tried it. Two surgeries and nine months of occupational therapy later, and here I am.

Pickleballs, like Wiffle balls, have holes all around them that allow for better accuracy and bounce. I don't know why this is, I'm not a scientist, but the holes are important and the game would be very different with a ball that doesn't have holes, for instance if you were playing pickleball with a bowling ball. "But Ellis," you say, "bowling balls *do* have holes." Those don't count. I learned that the hard way.

Look, I know it's fun to sit here and laugh about the ONE TIME I tried playing pickleball with a bowling ball; but let's move on, shall we?

The Court

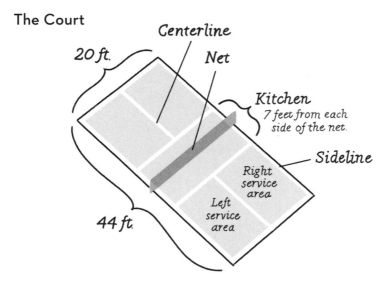

This is a diagram of a pickleball court.

It is about the size of a badminton court, or one-fourth the size of a tennis court. It's also about one sixty-fourth the size of a football field, but that isn't a helpful metric. Notice how each side of the pickleball court is divided into three zones: the right service court, the left service court and the non-volley zone, commonly referred to as "the kitchen." Why is it called the kitchen? That, my friend, is a story for another time.

Here's something you should know about me. When someone asks me a question and I answer "That, my friend, is a story for another time," it's because I have no idea what the answer is and I'm stalling. I don't know why it's called the kitchen! Nobody seems to know why it's called the kitchen! There are theories, however. Some people think it's a reference to the phrase "If you can't stand the heat, get out of the kitchen," or the lesser-known "If you can stand the heat, well, OH MY GOD MY KITCHEN IS ON FIRE!"

Another theory is that it's called the kitchen as a reference to shuffleboard. You see, since pickleball is a hybrid of a bunch of sports that are not shuffleboard, it only makes sense to take some of shuffleboard's jargon. We wouldn't want it to feel left out. In shuffleboard, the kitchen is a zone at the end of the table. If your puck lands there, you lose ten points.

"I had the kitchen redone!"

Why is *that* called the kitchen? That, my friend, is a story for another time.

The other important aspect of the court is the net. The net is important because it separates the teams, and it forces the players to keep the ball up in the air. Without the net, the game would be anarchy. Players would be crashing into one another, balls would be rolling around on the ground, sirens would go off, and people would be running around screaming, maybe starting fires. Yes, the net is what separates man from beast, civilized society from complete breakdown. If you really want to know what pickleball might be like without a net, check out my novel *Netless*, a gritty post-apocalyptic thriller set in a not-too-distant-future. It's scary stuff, and available on Amazon!

The Paddles

When it comes to hitting a pickleball back to your opponent, nothing beats the paddle. It's like it was made for doing just that. The pickleball paddle is bigger than a Ping-Pong paddle, and it is smooth on both sides. They have a range of weights, lighter giving more accuracy and heavier more force. A paddle is a personal choice, and it's best to try out a bunch before picking the one that's

"When you asked me to make some paddles,
I assumed you wanted to get a game going."

right for you. The connection you and your paddle have will be deep. You'll want to be with it at all times. Other people might not understand. They may say, "Hey, can you put that paddle down for one minute and help me with the groceries?" and you'll whisper, "No."

Oh! One second I just caught the waiter's eye—

Excuse me, excuse me, sir! I'm ready to order—

Ugh, never mind, he ignored me. Anyway, paddles are also responsible for one of the defining features of pickleball: the noise! Pickleball is a notoriously loud sport. The noise has been the source of drama for some neighborhoods and community centers. There have been lawsuits! Several of them! And I'm not even including the ones that I'm involved in. It's quite the controversy. The materials and design of the ball and paddle meet together for the perfect storm of noise in the form of a "pop!" I have been told that it's not exactly the level of the sound that is irksome, but the high pitch. People hate ongoing high-pitched noises. To test this theory, I screamed in a high pitch while my wife was asking me to help with the groceries. Much like the folks who live next to a pickleball court, she was not pleased. But a good writer must do his research at any cost.

"You mind keeping it down?"

Things You Don't Necessarily Need to Know but Probably Should

Singles/Doubles

How many friends do you have? One? Great, get on either side of the court and play some singles. Three? Get a game of doubles going! Two? That's more complicated. Have them fight to the death, victor gets to get in a few games. Zero? Why do you think that is? Is it because you're overly judgmental? Or maybe it's because of your bad politics, or general amoral philosophies on some important social issues? I mean, I don't know, this is just the vibe you give off on Twitter.

The Swing

Much like a novel has three acts, a good swing has three parts: the backswing, contact, and the follow-through. The backswing is like the setup to the action. Your arm is back, gripping the paddle, waiting for the ball. Anything might happen. There is so much mystery and intrigue. It's exciting, and you can't wait to see what happens next. Then comes act two—the contact. The ball hits the paddle. It's the culmination of all that setup. The action. The explosion. The spectacle. Wow. Then the follow-through. Your arm just sort of

"Great. Now we can't play doubles."

continues. The inevitable letdown. The realization that the author backed themselves into a corner, and no ending would be satisfying. So you get aliens, or a deus ex machina.

Everything was just a scene in a child's snow globe.

Your ball just hit the net.

"That's some follow-through."

Volley

A volley is when you hit the ball before it bounces in your side of the court. You are not allowed to do this in the kitchen. That's it. Not everything has to be a joke, OKAY? IS THAT OKAY WITH YOU?

Sorry. It's just that I have been sitting in this booth for almost half an hour, and the waiter is refusing to come over, and I'm getting a little cranky. I shouldn't have skipped breakfast.

The Dink Shot

The dink is a kind of shot where you hit the ball gently above the net, so that it lands on a low bounce in your opponent's kitchen, forcing them to run to the net in a desperate attempt to return it. You may have noticed that the title of this book is *Dink!* This is because pickleball players love the dink shot. It's all they talk about. Go up to any pickleball enthusiast and scream something like "OH MY GOD MY KITCHEN IS ON FIRE!" they'll respond, "My favorite shot is the dink!"

Things You Don't Need to Know, but What the Hell, Here They Are Anyway

Chainsaw Serve

Okay, I just put this in here because of the cool name. I mean, it's no Dink, but still. Chainsaw! BUZZZZ! Hell, yeah! You know what else is cool about it? The chainsaw serve is so badass that it's been banned. That's right, totally illegal in pickleball tournaments. Now, keep in mind that I have no idea what this move is or how to do it, but any illegal activity involving chainsaws is worth mentioning. If you want to see it in action, go out and rent the classic pickleball horror movie, *The Texas Chainsaw Serve Massacre*.

Tagging

This is when you intentionally hit an opponent with the ball! You see, if the ball hits you or any of your clothing, that's a fault and you lose the point, so folks purposefully try to "tag" opponents by hitting the ball at them as hard as possible. It can cause actual injury, so it is a controversial form of play, banned by some players. However, you can find lots of tagging if you dare to venture into the dark underbelly world of pickleball, where only the seediest of characters play. You can find these tournaments deep below pickleball clubs, behind locked doors. Knock three times and say the password: "It's Pickle Time!"

"Watch out for his chainsaw serve."

"By the way, I like to play with intentional tagging."

Coaching

This is when one player gives unsolicited advice to another player. Whether it's good advice or bad advice, it's very annoying, and if you are reading this, Uncle Leroy, I wish you would stop.

*"Strategically speaking,
your best move is to let him win."*

Dill Ball

A ball that has bounced once in the opposing court.

Falafel

A ball that has bounced weakly off your paddle and doesn't go far.

Flapjack

A shot that must bounce once before it can be hit.

Cheeseburger

Sorry, this isn't a pickleball term. It's from my lunch order. I'm so hungry.

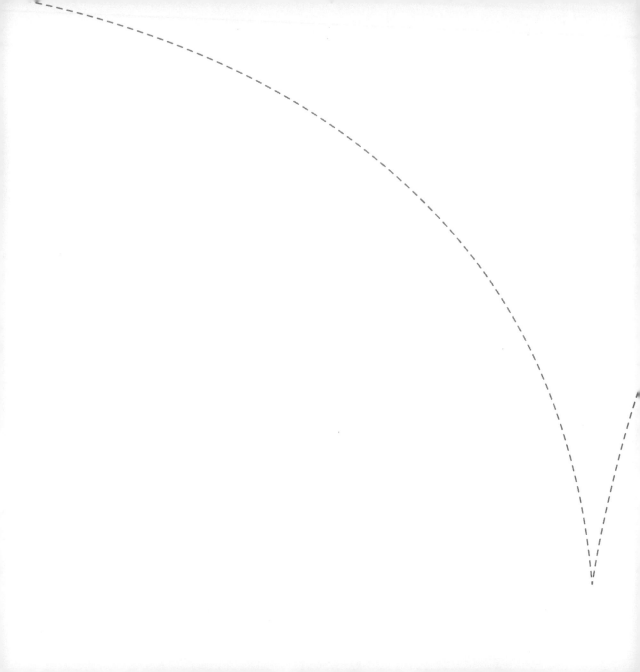

THE ORIGIN OF PICKLEBALL

The origin of pickleball is shrouded in mystery. Okay, that's not actually true, but I've always wanted to describe something as being "shrouded in mystery," and this might be my only chance. To be fair, the creation story of pickleball *is* a little confusing. I won't tell you more than that. Instead, I have devised a little game, if you will. I call it "Four Lies and a Truth." I'm still workshopping that. What I am going to present to you, dear reader, is five possible origins of the game of pickleball. Only one of them is true, and the others are common misconceptions or straight-up lies from the depths of my sick imagination. Will you be able to figure out which one is true? Put down your phone—googling is cheating! I shouldn't have to tell you that.

The Pickle-Boat Theory

It was the summer of 1965. Temperatures were soaring and radios were blasting "(I Can't Get No) Satisfaction" by the Rolling Stones. The place? Bainbridge Island, Washington. Joel Pritchard and Bill Bell were hanging out with their families, relaxing and enjoying the scraggily baritone of Mick Jagger. Everyone was having a blast. Well, almost everyone. Joel's son, Frank, who never could appreciate the hard-charging rock of the Stones, was bored. Joel sat his son down and said, "You think Mick Jagger ever gets bored? No! He uses his imagination and makes up things to do! Just like how I used to do, with my friends. When I was your age, we made up games!"

"Oh, yeah?" Frank replied. "Okay, then, why don't you make up a game right now?"

"Maybe I will!" Joel said in a huff and walked away. He got Bill, and together they went to the shed and grabbed a bunch of sports equipment: a Wiffle ball, a badminton net, and a bunch of table tennis paddles, and they made up a brand-new game. It was a hit, except for one problem: the table tennis paddles were just too darn small. So they walked down to their neighbor, Barney McCallum, and asked if he could whip up a few new paddles in the shed. Barney said, "Sure, no problem, and also have you heard this hit new song 'Satisfaction' by the Rolling Stones? It really pops!"

"It sure does!" said Joel and Bill, and together they all created the new paddles that are the basis of what we use today.

"This game is really great, but what do we call it?" asked Bill.

"Why not pickleball!" said Joan, Joel's wife. "You know, like a pickle boat—the last boat on a crew team that's comprised of who's left over, just like the equipment in this game!"

"That's a great idea!" Joel, Bill, and Barney said in unison. "Now, crank up that radio!"

The Dog Theory

It was the summer of 1965. Temperatures were soaring and radios were blasting "I Can't Help Myself (Sugar Pie, Honey Bunch)" by The Four Tops. The place? Bainbridge Island, Washington. Joel Pritchard and Bill Bell were hanging out with their families, relaxing and enjoying the mellow baritone of Levi Stubbs. Everyone was having a blast. Well, almost everyone. Joel's son, Frank, who never could appreciate the sweet harmony of The Four Tops, was bored. Joel sat his son down and said, "You think Levi Stubbs ever gets bored? No! He uses his imagination and makes up things to do! Just like how I used to do, with my friends. When I was your age, we made up games!"

"Oh, yeah?" Frank replied. "Okay, then, why don't you make up a game right now?"

"Maybe I will!" Joel said in a huff and walked away. He got Bill, and together they went to the shed and grabbed a bunch of sports equipment: a wiffle ball, a badminton net, and a bunch of table tennis paddles, and they made up a brand-new game. It was a hit, except for one problem: the table tennis paddles were just too darn small. So they walked down to their neighbor, Barney McCallum, and asked if he could whip up a few new paddles in the shed. Barney said, "Sure, no problem, and also have you heard this hit new song 'I Can't Help Myself (Sugar Pie, Honey Bunch)' by The Four Tops? It really pops!"

"It sure does!" said Joel and Bill, and together they all created the new paddles that are the basis of what we use today.

"This game is really great, but what do we call it?" asked Bill.

"Why not pickleball!" said Joan, Joel's wife. "You know, after our dog, Pickles!"

"Bark!" said Pickles the dog.

"That's a great idea!" Joel, Bill, and Barney said in unison. "Now, crank up that radio!"

The Ancient Alien Theory

It was the summer of 1965 BCE. Temperatures were soaring and musicians were blasting "Excerpt of Sumerian Hymn no. 14" by Anonymous Sumerian, circa 2000 BCE. The place? The City State of Ur, Ancient Mesopotamia. Two aliens, ZAXXIPHON and MAR-LAXX, OVERLORD OF THE COSMOS, were vacationing on Earth with their families, relaxing and enjoying the organized system of diatonic scales of Anonymous Sumerian. Everyone was having a blast. Well, almost everyone. ZAXXIPHON's son, Frank, who never could appreciate the stringed instruments in alternating fifths and fourths of Anonymous Sumerian, was bored. ZAXXIPHON sat his son down and said, "You think Anonymous Sumerian ever gets bored? No! He uses his imagination and makes up things to do! Just like how I used to do, with my friends. When I was your age, we made up games!"

"Oh, yeah?" Frank replied. "Okay, then, why don't you make up a game right now?"

"Maybe I will!" ZAXXIPHON said in a huff and walked away. He got MARLAXX, OVERLORD OF THE COSMOS, and together they went to the shed sector in their UFO and grabbed a bunch of sports equipment: a wiffle ball, a badminton net, and a bunch of table tennis paddles, and they made up a brand new game. It was a hit, except for one problem: the table tennis paddles were just too darn small. So, they beamed up to their neighbor, VVVZVZVZVZV, and asked if he could whip up a few new paddles in the shed sector of their UFO. VVVZVZVZVZV said, "Sure, no problem, and also have you heard this hit new song 'Excerpt of Sumerian Hymn no. 14' by Anonymous Sumerian? It really pops!"

"It sure does!" said ZAXXIPHON and MARLAXX, OVERLORD OF THE COSMOS, and together they all created the new paddles that are the basis of what we use today.

"This game is really great, but what do we call it?" asked MARLAXX, OVERLORD OF THE COSMOS.

"Why not pickleball!" said QUEEN OLRA of THE SEVEN MOONS, ZAXXIPHON's wife. "You know, after the sound our alien dog, ZALAXXXBORG, makes!"

"Pickleball!" said ZALAXXXBORG the alien dog.

"That's a great idea!" ZAXXIPHON, MARLAXX, OVERLORD OF THE COSMOS and VVVZVZVZVZV said in unison. "Now crank up that ancient lyre!"

The Time-Travel Theory

It was the summer of 2065. Temperatures were soaring from the radiation that the evil robots pumped into the atmosphere, and radios were blasting "SURRENDER HUMANS AND YOUR LIFE WILL BE SPARED" by the Robot Overlord. The place? An underground bunker beneath Bainbridge Island, Washington. Grayson Pritchard and Phoenix Bell were hanging out with their families, doing their best to survive while withstanding the constant onslaught of the robot laser fire. Everyone was scared, fearful of a future where the resistance would completely fall to the machine armies. Well, almost everyone. Grayson's son, Pickle, which is a perfectly normal name in the year 2065, was determined and hopeful. Joel sat his son down and said, "You think the Robot Overlord is going to get bored trying to kill us? No! He uses his imagination and makes up new horrible ways to torture humans! We're all doomed! Doomed!"

"No, we're not. We have one option left," Pickle replied. "All this time, I have been working on a new invention, and now it's done. Dad, I have created a time machine!"

"A time machine!" Grayson exclaimed. "Impossible!"

"It works, but I'll only have one chance to go back in time and prevent this future from happening."

"But how? Even if you could go back in time, how could you save us now?"

"I have a plan. I'm going to go back to 1965 and find my great-grandfather Joel. I'm going to persuade him to create a game. A game that is so fun and addicting that by the time it reaches peak popularity, humans and robots alike will bond over the sport and never go to war!"

"It might be just crazy enough to work!" Grayson said, and with that Pickle turned on the machine and disappeared in a blast of light.

It was the summer of 1965. Pickle raced to find his great-grandfather Joel, who was relaxing with his family.

"Joel!" said Pickle. "I am your great-grandson Pickle, and I have come from the future where humans are enslaved by evil robots who have taken over the world. I need your help. We need to create a new sport. One that will unite humans and robots 100 years from now."

"Whoa, whoa, slow down," said Joel. "Your name is Pickle?"

"It's a perfectly normal name in the year 2065," said Pickle.

"Understood," said Joel; "let's get to work." So Joel and Pickle and Joel's buddy Bill, who was just rolling with it, got together and went to the shed and grabbed a bunch of sports equipment: a Wiffle ball, a badminton net, and a bunch of table tennis paddles, and made up a brand-new game. It was a hit, except for one problem: the table tennis paddles were just too darn small. So, they walked down to their neighbor, Barney McCallum, and asked if he could whip up a few new paddles in the shed. Barney said, "Sure, no problem, and also have you heard these hit new songs 'Satisfaction' by the Rolling Stones and 'I Can't Help Myself (Sugar Pie, Honey Bunch)' by The Four Tops? Both of them really pop!"

"No," said Pickle. "Music has been outlawed in 2065. The only sound I know is the constant shrieks of human suffering."

Everyone sort of looked around, trying not to make eye contact with Pickle.

"Anyway, this game is really great, but what do we call it?" asked Bill.

"Why not pickleball!" said Joan, Joel's wife. "You know, after Pickle, the man who saved humanity! And also our dog, Pickles."

"Bark!" said Pickles.

"That's a great idea!" Joel, Bill, and Barney said in unison. "Now crank up that radio!"

"I'm honored!" said Pickle, but no one heard him because the radio was playing so loudly. He then disappeared back to his own time, which was now a utopian paradise where robots and humans played pickleball all day every day, and everyone enjoyed the catchy beats of the Rolling Stones and the Four Tops, as well as a whole bunch of other bands I never mentioned.

The Vampire Theory

The exact same story as the others but with vampires.

The Answer

So, which is the true story? Well, if you watch the History Channel, you'll definitely find some folks who believe the ancient aliens theory. The vampire theory, as richly detailed as it was, is not correct either. Is it the dog story, the one where the game is named after the dog Pickles? No! In fact, that's a common misconception. The dog, who came after the game was invented, was in fact named after the game! That leaves two possibilities: the time-travel theory and the pickle-boat theory.

You're not going to believe it, but in fact the pickle-boat theory is the real story. I know it sounds unbelievable—I mean, who knows random facts about crew teams, much less names a game after it?—but it's true! That's the story of how pickleball got its name. So next time someone asks you if you know how pickleball got its name, you can say "Yes!" and then they can say, "Oh, okay then," and you can both sit in silence, thinking about what to talk about next.

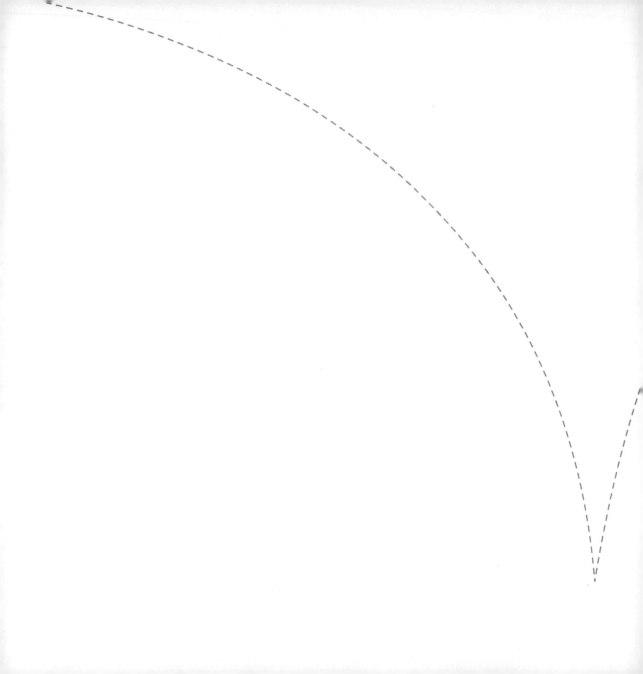

HISTORICAL PICKLEBALL DIAGRAMS

Although pickleball was officially created in the mid-1960s, there is historical evidence that earlier versions of the game have appeared since the late Stone Age. The following examples are a few of the more prominent examples of where pickleball has been depicted before the twentieth century.

All images and information were provided by the American Historical Association for Pickleball Enthusiasts, or AHAPE.

Cave Paintings

The first historical record of pickleball was discovered by speleologists in 1994 in a cave in Florida. These drawings were painted by peoples somewhere between 30,000 and 35,000 years ago. They seem to indicate an alternative to hunting, in which the losers would be eaten by the winners.

Viking Runestone

This boulder engraving can be dated back to 1060 CE. It depicts a large warrior opposite a pickleball court from a beast, possibly the mythological wolf Fenrir. The inscription reads: "This monument is for Vingmund, a lousy warrior, but fierce on the court." This rune-stone is also evidence that Vikings landed in North America, as it was found in south Florida.

Leonardo da Vinci's Lost Notebook

A recently uncovered notebook from Leonardo da Vinci features a diagram for a game he calls "palla di sottaceti." It shows his plans to create a pickleball court, racket, and ball, and some notes on where in Italy it can be installed. The entire notebook itself is an interesting artifact. It was made during Leonardo's recently discovered journey to the New World, and the pickleball entry was most likely drawn while he was in what is now Florida.

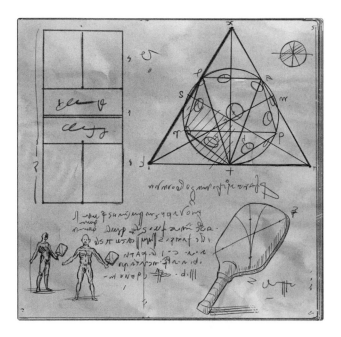

Projected Map of the United States, 2060

A map of the United States based on ecological and cultural shifts.

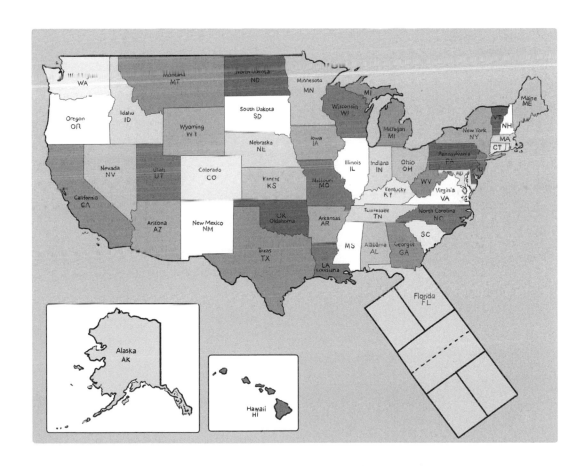

Cartoon Interlude 2

"*There are worse places to be beached.*"

"I'm not surprised to find this. You can fit a pickleball court anywhere."

"Ok, Ok! The ball wasn't out!"

"He's really good. He's an omnipotent being that has existed before time and the universe, plus he used to play tennis."

"Aye, the pain was like none other. I yelled in agony, cursing the heavens for my misfortune. And that, friend, is the story of how I sprained my ankle playing pickleball."

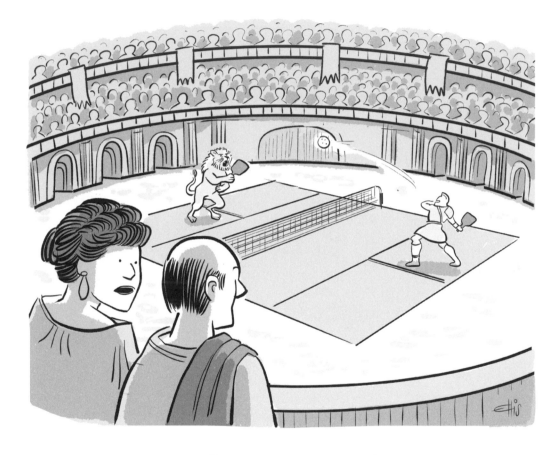

"Well, now I'm entertained."

"I draw the line at Cornichon Ball."

LAMENT OF A TENNIS BALL

Well, well, kid. Look at you. Pickleball, the new hot game in town. Feels good, doesn't it? Having your name on everyone's lips? I remember when the only thing folks would talk about was tennis. The nonstop buzz, the magazine articles, the red-carpet interviews. "Tennis Ball! I love your color, is that neon yellow? Tennis Ball, tell us, is it true you and Baseball are dating?" Sure, the paparazzi are annoying, but it's a small price to pay for the kind of fame only a Football is accustomed to.

Boy, do I have stories. There was that time Venus, Serena, and I hit the bars in downtown LA, drank all night, and ended up playing doubles with Madonna and Carrot Top until 6 a.m. Or that time Mats Wilander hit me so high, I flew over the court and landed in a martini glass being held by Mayor Ed Koch! I got olive juice all over his new thousand-dollar suit. Let me tell you, it was hard talking my way out of that one! But later that night, Wilander and I just laughed and laughed. *Sigh*. Those days are behind me. It's you everyone wants to party with now.

Ha. Those were fun times, but at the end of the day nothing beat the rush of feeling my fuzz blowing in the wind.

Take some advice from an old ball: enjoy the spotlight, but stay grounded and focused. Brackets, statistics, rankings—that's all a distraction. You just keep your eye on yourself and don't get caught up in the numbers. I mean, take Basketball. Every March he succumbs to madness. People get excited, but the reality is just depressing.

And hey—don't forget you're part of a team. It may be called "pickle*ball*," but you would go nowhere without the racket. I know balls and sticks usually keep their distance, but there's a mutual respect that needs to be maintained. You get most of the attention, so it's up to you to maintain the relationship. Check up on it every now and then. Send a nice letter. Don't forget its birthday. Compliment it on its cool graphics. That kind of thing. If that relationship goes south, you better believe it's game, set, and match.

Take breaks. You can't be on the court 24/7. I've seen balls pop from too much pressure. I once saw a football work hard all season only to deflate during the Super Bowl. The press would have you believe it was that poor equipment manager, but we sports balls know the truth: he just couldn't take it. So keep in shape, sure, but don't neglect your mental health.

You don't have to be so serious all the time! The game will have it ups and downs: you have to learn to just be a sport and roll with it.

Make sure to brush up on your sports analogies. Sure, "We need a Hail Mary" and "the ball's in your court" are great, but familiarize yourself with some of the lesser-known ones. You know, like "It's on the tip of my Lacrosse Stick," and "You're acting like a real floppy discus." It makes you sound more professional.

Be creative. Change up the game every now and then. No one wants to see you toss the same ideas back and forth. Take a cue from Eight Ball: he always has some new ideas in the pocket. And if one of your ideas doesn't fly? Well, like Baseball always says, sometimes life is just a swing and a miss.

Most of all, stay humble. Don't bounce too close to the sun. Remember the little balls that helped you along the way: Ping-Pong Ball and Shuttlecock never really got their chance to shine, but regardless of that, they saw something in you and they lifted you out of obscurity. And Willie Ball. I know you two don't always see eye-to-eye, but you have more in common than you might think. Be kind. One day when you fall from grace—and that day will come—you're going to need friends.

Before you know it, a new sport will come along and start to steal the spotlight from you. Maybe some wild new hybrid of soccer and handball. Maybe it will have some crazy name, like yours. Burgerball, or Ham and Turkey on Rye Disc, or something. Don't let jealousy stop you from helping them out. They may have some crazy new look, with some silly name, and you might think "they'll never last," but anything can happen in the wide world of sports, and you can't stop a home run once it's out of the stadium. Believe me, I never would have thought I would see the day that they started tearing up tennis courts to make way for the likes of *you*, but here we are. Was I jealous? Of course.

I mean, you're not even in the Olympics and these retirement homes in Florida think they can just get rid of *me*? ME! TENNIS! A SPORT THAT HAS CAPTIVATED FANS FROM AROUND THE WORL—

Ahem. Sorry. What I'm trying to say, kid, is that your moment is here, so enjoy it. You're a good kid, silly but professional. You play well and you make people happy. That's the most important thing. The smile on an athlete's face when they score a point for the home team. If you remember that, you'll be good.

All right, enough from this old ball. I'll let you get back to it. See you around, kid. Keep flying high over that net, or . . . as high as you can. My god, you are a gentle sport.

PICKLEBALL:
DO's AND DON'Ts

---

kay, here we go! Into the weeds! The technical stuff. We got your pickleball dos and we got your pickleball don'ts. We do not have any pickleball maybes. That's wishy-washy nonsense, and who has time for wishy-washy nonsense in this economy? Not me.

Just in case you're not sure how a "do" and "don't" section works, basically *do* do the "do's" and *do not do* the "don'ts." Do all that; do not not do all that. If you do happen to not do that, and you do the don'ts and don't do the do's, then you got your do's and don'ts mixed up and you'll have to redo your do's and redon't your don'ts. Try not to redo your don'ts and redon't your do's. That's a classic mistake.

In summary: Do do do's, do do no don'ts, don't not do do's, don't not do no don'ts, redo do's if you don't do them and redon't don'ts if you do do them. I hope that clears up any confusion.

"Excellent composition. Terrible form."

DO: Use the dink shot early and often.

DON'T: Only use the dink. Remember to vary your shots.

DO: Keep good form. Relax your shoulders, keep your back straight, feet at shoulder width apart and knees slightly bent, and keep your paddle up at around your chest.

DON'T: Flawless triple Lutz to double axel, ending in a catch foot layback spin.

DO: Take small, well-balanced steps.

DON'T: Warm up and stretch before a game. No, wait, that's a "DO." I guess these are both "DO's."

DO: Keep your grip on the paddle loose.

DON'T: Keep your grip too tight on the paddle. Okay, I'm just realizing now that this is redundant.

DO: Hit lobs strategically when your opponent isn't expecting it.

DON'T: Forget to bring in the groceries. (Sorry—this is just a note for me.)

DO: Master the third shot drop.

DON'T: Get distracted on your phone all day like last week when I was supposed to get a lot done but then I got sucked into a YouTube video series called "How to master the third shot drop."

DO: Aim the ball at your opponent's feet.

DON'T: Get caught up in your opponent's footwear. Yes, they are nice shoes, but you can talk about it after the game.

DO: Focus on the game. Try not to get distracted by catchy songs that might be playing nearby.
DON'T: Stop belieeeeeving....

DO: Wear the right shoes while playing pickleball.
DON'T: Forget to clean your dress shoes, since you wore them last time you were playing pickleball, instead of wearing the proper shoes, which you couldn't find. Since we're here, don't forget to put your pickleball shoes away in a place you will remember!

DO: Get to the net early and quickly.
DON'T: Stay too deep in the court during the whole game. Again, this is redundant. I apologize for that.

DO: Communicate with your partner. I don't know if I meant this as a pickleball thing, or like a tip to keep a healthy marriage.
DON'T: Impinge on your partner's space. Again, not sure how I meant this. I guess you can apply it to what's appropriate for your situation.

DO: "Prabice lurc geerse" ??
DON'T: Write so illegibly you can't even read your own handwriting.

DO: "Practice your serve!" That's what I wrote. See? That little squiggly line is an *s*, not a *g*.
DON'T: . . . and the *c* and the *t* in *Practice* formed together to look like a *b*.

DO: Serve underhand, diagonally cross-court.
DON'T: Serve underhand, diagonally cross court while playing basketball.

DO: Use the dink shot early and often. Did I say that already? I'm losing track.
DON'T: Make these lists go on so long that you run out of jokes.

DO: Serve underhand.
DON'T: (Remember to add a joke here when you come up with another one.)

Cartoon Interlude 3

"My wife is obsessed with pickleball. It's starting to scare me."

"Now if he'll just swallow one more paddle, we'll be set."

"No mention of her serve."

"Oh, no, it's not a problem at home. We need
help with communication on the court."

"I have my knee braces, ankle braces,
wrist bands . . . did I forget anything?"

"Too bad you didn't awake from uneasy dreams to find yourself transformed into a better pickleball player!"

*"I should have warned you—pickleball
makes you work up a sweat."*

An Apology

Dear Reader,

I would like to apologize for the cartoon you just read. It was an attempt to make a joke about how pickleball can make people work up a sweat, but upon retrospect it was not funny, it was just very gross. When I started this book I knew that I would have to come up with 40+ pickleball cartoons. I thought I could do it, but when I hit fifteen I started to run out of ideas. The pressure got to me and my usual standards dropped; hence this cartoon. Just to be clear: sweat is gross. Swimming in a pool of sweat that comes up to your waist is gross. Being surrounded by so much sweat, both yours and someone else's, flowing everywhere— probably getting a little in your mouth—is gross. It's not pleasant thinking about it, and I'm sorry I put that imagery in your head.

I hope the rest of the cartoons in this book will meet your approval, or at the very least that they won't involve gallons and gallons of human sweat.

Best,
Ellis

PICKLEBALL AT THE MOVIES

Pickleball is on the verge of making it big-time. It's America's fastest-growing sport (did I mention that yet?), and it's got major athletic sportswear sponsors and popular tournaments. It's even on track to become part of the Olympics. But so far, it's missing one necessary element to be considered a major sport: its very own Major Motion Picture. All the big-time sports have movies made about them. *Moneyball, Any Given Sunday,*

"I don't suppose you play pickleball?"

Bend It Like Beckham, The Hunger Games. But pickleball has yet to make its debut on the silver screen. No need to worry, though, I'm here to help get that ball rolling.

Imagine, if you will, that you are a hot-shot Hollywood movie executive looking for your next big movie to wow audiences across the country. And it just so happens you are stuck in an elevator with me, the guy who is full of ideas for the next big movie, and *they're all pickleball-related.* I hope you like lots of money, because these are billion-dollar ideas. You can stop hitting the buttons over and over again: this elevator is not going anywhere.

Pitch 1: The Dinkling Lot

The Shining meets *The Sandlot*, but with pickleball!

Everyone knows the classic Stanley Kubrick horror flick *The Shining*. It's got memorable lines, tense camera angles, foreboding music, and a very naturalistic performance from Jack Nicholson. And who doesn't love *The Sandlot*, the story of a group of kids who love baseball and deal with their shared trauma caused by their next-door neighbor's dog? America loves those movies, so

"Come play doubles with us, Danny."

how could America not love *The Dinkling Lot*, the story of Danny Smalls, a young boy who tries to join a local pickleball team comprised of a ragtag group of rowdy kids? When Danny accidently hits their prized pickleball into their neighbor's haunted house, he must face his fears and retrieve the ball from the pickleball-loving ghosts that dwell within. It's a horrific bloodbath pickleball flick that you can bring the whole family to!

Pitch 2: Mission Pickle Dog

Mission: Impossible meets *Air Bud*, but with pickleball!

To infiltrate a terrorist organization intent on polluting the world with a deadly pathogen one pickleball tournament at a time, Agent Buddy "Pickles" Hunt, a purebred Golden Retriever, must go undercover as a ranked pickleball player and discover the madman behind it all. Although his presence causes some controversy among hardcore fans, there's nothing in the rulebook that says a secret-agent dog can't play pickleball. Can Pickles stop the bad guys in time, or will he get sucked into his new persona, focusing only on becoming the top dog in pickleball?

Pitch 3: The Pickleball Cinematic Universe

Okay, this is not so much one movie as it is a series of innumerable interconnected movies and television shows that span the next twenty years through various franchises. You wouldn't be able to understand one movie without seeing any of the others, forcing viewers to watch and rewatch the collected media dozens of times. It combines America's two favorite things: pickleball and homework. The plots of these movies don't really matter: take the top dozen pickleball players, give them powers, make them play against a bunch of pickleball-hating aliens. Add colorful explosions and an onslaught of cheeky fourth-wall-breaking quips for the actors to say as they wink at the audience, their disdain for the material visually palpable. This stuff writes itself.

"You have to fly me up there! I'm the only one
who can help Godzilla with his form!"

Pitch 4: Add Pickleball to Any Franchise

Listen, I'm not going to overstate it here, just add pickleball to your next planned sequel or reboot to whatever nostalgia-ridden franchise you've got going on at the moment. *Godzilla v. Kong: Court Side. Lord of the Rings: Return of the Swing. 007: Live and Let Dink.* Hell, force Harrison Ford at gunpoint to do *Indiana Jones and The Paddle of Doom.* I don't know, you're the movie executive in this scenario, you tell me.

Pitch 5: Art House Pickleball Movie

Pickleball, but it's like a metaphor for something.

"Oh, that's for later in the interview process."

PICKLEBALL QUIZ

You're far enough along in this book that I think it's time you tested your skills. What you see next is the ultimate pickleball quiz, unless of course you take another one after this. Be warned: I'm not going to take it easy on you just because this is a humor book. No way. In fact, I'm going to make it extra-hard to make up for all the silliness that came before. So roll up your sleeves, and don't get distracted by that funny mole on your arm that your sleeve was just covering, because here we go!

1. Which is an actual rule in pickleball?

   a. There should be one bounce per side.

   b. There should be two bounces per side.

   c. There should be one bounce per alternate side,
   11 a.m. to 2 p.m. on Tuesdays and Fridays.

   d. There should be one bounce per side in the loading zone
   only, 8 a.m. to 5 p.m.; violators may be subject to fines.

2. True or False? Pickleball can be played with two or four people, and also you owe me fifty bucks.

   a. True

   b. False

3. The non-volley zone is also known as the:

   a. Basement

   b. Living room

   c. Kitchen

   d. That little room under the stairs that you think you can keep your vacuum in, but it's actually too small, and what the hell am I supposed to do with this little room?

4. Pickleball is primarily made up of which three sports:

   a. Badminton, Ping-Pong, and shuffleboard

   b. Badminton, Ping-Pong, and tennis

   c. Badminton, Ping-Pong, and table tennis

   d. Whatever is currently on ESPN, whatever is currently on ESPN2, and whatever is currently on C-SPAN

5. True or False? Pickleball is my aunt's favorite sport.

    a. True

    b. False

6. What is the maximum amount of holes in an outdoor pickleball?

    a. 17

    b. 4

    c. 40

    d. All of the above

7. Which of the following is NOT true?

    a. Pickleball was created in 1965.

    b. Pickleball has its own national governing body, the United States of America Pickleball Association.

    c. A house cat is genetically 95.6% tiger. (I said "true," I didn't specify that it had to be true about pickleball.)

    d. Pickleball was named after the family pet, Pickles.

8. A volley is:

   a. When you hit the ball without letting it bounce.

   b. When the ball is hit back and forth over the net.

   c. When the ball is hit out of bounds.

   d. A low area of land between hills or mountains, typically with a river or stream flowing through it.

9. A dink shot is:

   a. When the ball is hit high and deep into the opponents' court, forcing them to retreat.

   b. A small drink of distilled Dink Brand liquor.

   c. When the ball is softly hit into the opponent's non-volley zone, forcing them to approach the net.

   d. When the ball is hit over your head and down into your opponent's court with a lot of force.

10. Fill in the blank: "Pickleball is America's __ growing sport."

    a. Fastest

    b. Alarmingly

    c. Dangerously

    d. Deadliest

11. The author of this book is

    a. Handsome and intelligent

    b. Charming and witty

    c. The person you owe fifty bucks to

    d. All of the above

12. A train leaves Grand Central Station at 6 p.m. heading north at an average speed of eighty-five miles per hour; at the same time another train departs, heading in the opposite direction at an average speed of 120 miles per hour. If these trains start exactly 1,500 miles apart, how long until they collide? I'm now realizing that this isn't a pickleball question. I don't want to think up a new question, so just pretend the trains are filled with pickleballs or something.

Cartoon Interlude 4

"No, I don't think it's pickleball elbow."

"For the love of god, keep your eye on the ball!"

HOW THE FEUD STARTED

"Hatfield, old buddy, want to play?"

"Looks like we have time for one more game."

"Let's figure out who the better player is, then
keep the ball away from them."

"Let's divide the teams into
back pain vs. leg pain."

"Little help?"

Acknowledgments

The author (me, I'm the author; Ellis is my name) would first and foremost like to thank his family. Meghan, Sadie, Max, Mom, Dad, Lev, Chris, Aunt Goldy, John, Janae, Matt, Rachel, David, Mary, Paul and any secret relatives I may not know about, thanks for enabling and inspiring me to write silly nonsense all day. All my love to you.

Next, the author (again, that's me, Ellis) would like to thank his agent Joy Tutela, his editors Kate Zimmermann and Jay Sacher, as well as his cartoon editors Emma Allen, Colin Stokes, and Bob Mankoff. Also, many thanks to the book's go-to pickleball expert, Mike Crosby.

Finally, the author (you guessed it, it's still Ellis) would like to thank the following group of friends who have read, reread, made suggestions, added jokes, advised, informed, encouraged, and discouraged this book. I appreciate all their time and energy and generally just dealing with all my crap. They are (in no particular order): Johny DiNapoli, Lars Kenseth, Asher Perlman, Sofia Warren, Navied Mahdavian, Brendan Loper, Amy Kurzweil, Kendra Allenby, Jason Adam Katzenstein, David Ostow, Jerald Lewis, Hilary Campbell, Chantel Tattoli, Ben Frisch, and Tom Chitty. Thanks so much, everyone. I owe you all fifty bucks.

But good luck getting it out of me.

About the Author

The first thing you should know about the author is that his name is Ellis Rosen. The second thing you should know is that he's almost six foot three inches. Also, Rosen is not a professional pickleball player by any means, but he is a cartoonist, writer, and illustrator living in Brooklyn. His cartoons appear regularly in *The New Yorker*. He has also had work in *The New York Times*, *MAD Magazine*, *The Washington Post*, and *Wired*. He is the co-editor of the cartoon anthology "Send Help!" and has a weekly cartoon series, "Junk Drawer," at gocomics.com. He's got a mother who can often be found on Goodreads.

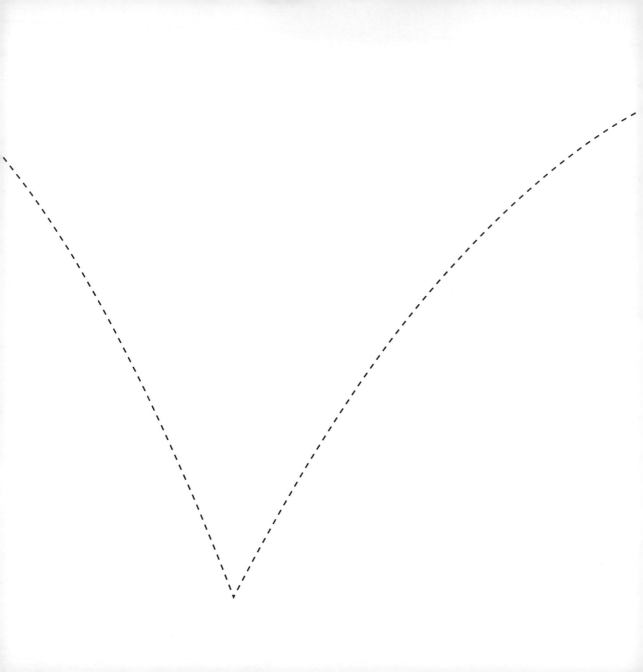